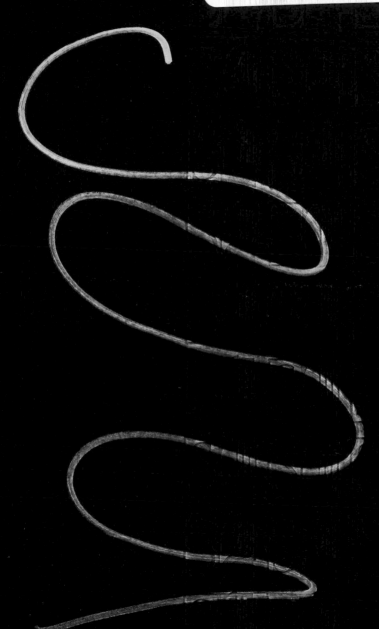

THE NIGHT WE'RE NOT SLEEPING IN

◆ ◆ ◆

Sean Bishop

◆ ◆ ◆

WINNER OF THE 2013 KATHRYN A. MORTON PRIZE IN POETRY
SELECTED BY SUSAN MITCHELL

Sarabande Books

LOUISVILLE, KENTUCKY

◆ ◆ ◆

MANAGING EDITOR
SARABANDE BOOKS, INC.
2234 DUNDEE ROAD, SUITE 200
LOUISVILLE, KY 40205

◆ ◆ ◆

Library of Congress Cataloging-in-Publication Data

Bishop, Sean, 1983–
The night we're not sleeping in / Sean Bishop.
pages cm
Summary: "The 2013 Kathryn A. Morton Prize in Poetry Selected by Susan
Mitchell"—Provided by publisher.
ISBN 978-1-936747-93-1 (paperback)
I. Title.
PS3602.I765N54 2014
811'.6—dc23
2014010254

◆ ◆ ◆

Book design & cover art by Sean Bishop.

◆ ◆ ◆

MANUFACTURED IN CANADA.
THIS BOOK IS PRINTED ON ACID-FREE PAPER.

◆ ◆ ◆

Sarabande Books is a nonprofit literary organization.
The Kentucky Arts Council, the state arts agency,
supports Sarabande Books with state tax dollars
and federal funding from the National Endowment for the Arts.

for my father

CONTENTS

FOREWORD

Sean Bishop's *The Night We're Not Sleeping In* is a book equal to our dark and savage world. It rages, it defies, it rebels. It spits bile—brilliantly, refusing all the palliatives that religions, philosophies, and the various isms have proffered for centuries. Like Achilles, Bishop has a muscular capacity for anger. Like Milton's Satan he will not be broken in spirit. Like Beowulf, given a choice between grief and rage, he will choose rage. Rage over the very nature of what it means to be human: to suffer and to inflict pain. *The Night We're Not Sleeping In* is not a book that will comfort. Like all great art, it will disturb and provoke its readers.

As poet, Bishop also reminds me of another heroic figure: Odysseus insisting he be tied to the mast of his ship so that he can listen to the dangerous song of the Sirens. What Bishop listens to is the dangerous singing inside himself, which is also the dangerous singing outside himself: the cruel, barbaric music of humanity. Bishop's masterful poems are remarkable for their capacity to sustain disturbing realities. Unlike Milton's Adam, who collapses when the Angel Michael squeezes drops into his eyes that allow him to see far into the future the consequences of his actions, Bishop keeps looking; and because of the power of his figurative language, what he sees the reader will also see.

Of course, rage is not a simple emotion, and Bishop's rage is a cocktail of bitterness, betrayal, hurt, regret, disillusionment—and, above all, grief, which, in the last poems of the book, breaks through finally with such force, this reader was shattered into cathartic sobs of relief. Bishop is intellectually and emotionally complex, a poet fully conscious of the shadow side—his and ours—which he articulates with fast-moving jabs of insight.

In *The Night We're Not Sleeping In* three poetic sequences dialogue with and interrupt each other. One six-poem sequence follows Adam,

Bishop's Everyman, in his journey from innocence ("Adam Before the Advent of Psychiatry") through experience ("Adam Reports from the Distant Future"); another sequence of six poems includes Bishop's potential readers, referred to as "Secret Fellow Sufferers." A third sequence harrows with Bishop's personal losses. All these poems are daring, even heroic, because without flinching, they follow emotional experiences to their disturbing climaxes. "Adam Home from the Wars" begins with a jaunty ballad-like song,

> Yes, when the orchard's dolled up in pastels
> and the finches scrawl cursive across the sky
> and the big moon sags like a tit o'er the meadows,
> I'll trade in my Glock for a pocket of dew.

but ends several stanzas later with,

> I made for my wound a poultice of wounds
> and the ones I wounded made poultices too.
> We've come here this evening to give them to you.

Only a master of mixed diction would place that romantic "o'er" after "tit," or use "Glock" and "dew" in the same line; only a master craftsman would choose for those chilling last lines a rhyme that echoes the innocent-sounding "pocket of dew" of the opening stanza; and only a poet with deep insight into human nature would understand how we bandage ourselves with the wounds we inflict on others. Reading a great book is risky because you will not be the same person when you have finished it. You will have lost your innocence. *The Night We're Not Sleeping In* is a great book. It will disturb and provoke you into the experience of reading it again—and again. A dark music that rages and grieves in your ears what you finally come to realize is the almost unbearable song of yourself.

—*Susan Mitchell*

Terms of Service

The signed agrees to breath, to the lungs' soggy bellows.

To night's eight-hour wake, the little deaths of sleeping-with.

To drink. To eat at predictable intervals.

And grow hair. And grow wiser. And gimpy. And old.

The signed agrees to like ice cream. To unfold
himself at dawn for coffee in the nook.

To possess a collection of books, beach-worn
by occasional, brief vacations.

The signed shall keep his firearms in a discreet location.
Shall wait for the guests to leave to weep.
Shall reflect serenely each dusk on his stoop
when the sun splashes rorschachs on the roadside gravel.

Should the signed become 'anxious,' 'unhappy,' or 'rattled';
should his service be tampered with or otherwise interrupted
by means including but not limited to mugging,
meningitis, advanced interrogation, or having his heart
plucked and chewed like a fig by Roxanne,

the signed shall strive to remain in compliance
with his duties, to venture bravely forward, to understand

that, irrespective of the signed or the contracting company,

some people may depart without notice,
packing their things in the night,
leaving only their hair pins on the windowsills.

Furthermore should the signed's father choke in his sleep,
should his brother spoon down a brown bottle of pills,
should his mother succumb to the village of tumors
thatching their damp huts inside her,

the signed shall hold harmless said company
for adjusting the terms of the Family Plan.

As a courtesy in such cases the company may reveal itself
through flocks of oddly colored birds that land
to hold parliament in the backyard oak,
or doors slamming, unprovoked,
at a meaningful hour of night.

The company shall not be held liable
should the signed fail to recognize said communications.

In return for the signed's full cooperation,
the company consents to buoy the signed
from his dreams each morning until such time
as it deems this contract has been fulfilled.

When it comes to pass that the signed is killed
or his heart stutters out like a wind-up toy,

it shall be understood that the signed is owed
no resigned joy, no otherworldly will,
no light-beam propped on a long bank of clouds.

Though such comforts, if provided
by the signed, shall be allowed.

1

Adam Before the
Advent of Psychiatry

The first dark arrived I got scared so I died.
Died when I saw the desert,
when the first fig passed like a fist   ·
through my guts.

        And was risen. And was risen
as a cat toy limp on its string is risen
and torn down again by its bored lord's bite.

I jumped from the mountain. I breathed
in the far swamp's muddy tea. I jabbed
a bear with a stick until it ate me—but woke
brand new among the bruised fruits
of my organs.

        It became a kind of hobby: falling
on a spear, climbing the highest tree
when the lightning stitched the clouds
to the night behind it, wearing the snakes
like poisonous scarves, or making
a midnight snack of my arm.

        I got listless. The lord
stopped listening. Now and then:
an odd shape on the waves, a slight sigh
among the pines, until the only proof
was waking beside the remains
of yesterday's body, alive.

A Bit of Forgiveness

Dear fat sagacious angels in the cumular eaves, why is it
that today, eating pork chops of all things, I'm thinking
of the time I stabbed Phil Kimble with an oak branch I whittled,
for no good reason? I must have been ten. I must have been
that age when a little boy's brain first stews
in a broth of Testosterone and Stupid,
until all its should-have-knowns unglue.

       In my town there were the boys
who took the walleyed girl to the woods
to do things she couldn't say. And there was a girl
who arrived to school one day with the stove's red coils
mapping both of her palms. And so I stabbed my friend,
Phil Kimble, with an oak branch I whittled:
a boy so much like me that sometimes my father
would call him by my name. A boy I loved as closely
as a father allows two boys to love. Filled as he was
with vague wonders, I guess I wanted to know
what a thing like me was made of—to hear his choked "oh"
when the point broke through, or to see the dough-boy
white of his cheeks when his mom rushed out
to wrench the branch from my hands.

       Dear honorable ma'ams
and sirs of the jury, forgive the barn burner
his love of the match. Forgive the knife its love
of the wind-felled branch, and the human

8

animal its love of the pig animal. Dear Phil,
I'm writing you now to say that the pork chops
were delicious, that I thought of you today
while eating them, and that I don't know why
I stabbed you, really, except maybe because
I wanted to poke a small window
into the piñata of myself. Phil, forgive
the awful metaphor. Forgive me, Phil.

Reading Dante in the ICU

Today I'd like to talk for a while about death
among the gift shop's plush koalas and chrysanthemums,
its aisles and aisles of light-dazed kittens

pouting from cards. Upstairs a surgeon
is drilling a hole in my father's brain,
and what pours forth when the burr pulls out

could be a sort of anthem
for the miracle-believers of the world—more likely
it will just be blood. So many cards. So many

get-well cats in stethoscopes, dressed as nurses,
white inside. If I tell you, now, that once
I had to kill a mewling thing like these

because its back was a corkscrew, broken
by someone else's boot, would you think
I'd shown it mercy? Would you think I'd been humane?

By now, the surgeon is telling his assistant
that sometimes the way out is through, in these cases:
when the drill punches in, the patient comes to,

as if he'd trekked back to the maze-like places
of youth, or the womb, and just needed a space
to escape through. In hell,

says Dante, there is just such a space,
although no one ever finds it—
so some of the dead must do

what they refused to do in life, forever,
while others must do the things they did, over
and over again. In an hour or two

the surgeon will call me in, and frown,
and smooth his green gown, and give me
the odds. And then I'll be left to the hoses

inflating my father with breath. Some things
I've done in this world I know
I'll have to do again.

Adam Explains
His Implications

There's a hole in your tin pail, that's what I mean.
I mean you wear it—I mean you're a breakable
mini-anyone, playing soldier, squinting through it
at your father whom you hate.

What I mean is that's you at the barbecue,
burning the burgers. That's you
mowing the wet lawn, choking the blade.

There is a piece of you, I mean,
that you adore, that wanders loose
and ruins everything, and whatever

you make—an omelet, a bracelet
from a dandelion stem, a dreamed-up someone
with complementary sex parts
by whom you judge all prospects—

will wear your face against your wishes
and need to be destroyed.

I mean you are mud-made
and daily trample yourself.

I mean, put some clothes on.

I mean there are things you don't want to know,
and although the world is there
without you—although

the black wasps jitter in their holes
whether you tell them to or not—

each morning you rise and bend the world
by naming it. If you call the boy or girl
beside you, who yesterday did God knows what
with whom, laughing in the bushes,
Love, then that is love.

Adam Home from the Wars

Yes, when the orchard's dolled up in pastels
and the finches scrawl cursive across the sky
and the big moon sags like a tit o'er the meadows,
I'll trade in my Glock for a pocket of dew.

And the wars will stop. And everyone
will do the dishes. And the lion
will sweetly go down on the lamb
as among the rifle casings the brambles
eject—at last—their thorns.

Once, on a bench by the river, the little ducks
seemed bread-sated and happy. I had my girl.
It was the Great Past Tense and everything was lovely.

Then, on the breeze: burnt spruce or a musk
of black powder and blood from a further field.

I made for my wound a poultice of wounds,
and the ones I wounded made poultices too.
We've come here this evening to give them to you.

Here's to Killing

Here's to killing. Here's to screeching
rubber-burned through happy standers-by,
to the bomb like a small sun
born above the city. Here's to murder,

manslaughter, the lexicon of –cides: where Cain
slinks back from the lamb-specked pasture,
a prince goes epileptic over bitter wine, or a boy
drops the gun by his wound-bleached mother.

Here's to the noose, to the mortar, to the spear
so patient in its palm-draped pit,
to the death ray arriving from a distant planet
to melt the trees into brownish scum. Friends,

here's to killing—not because it's fun
but because the days fill up with static,
because the limbs go numb from sitting,
because anyway we can't run

from the inside-out gas creeping through the city
or the tumors that swallow our bowels as we sleep—
because, at last, we must succumb. And so
we have a duty: To break. To bleed. To go

quietly dumb in our book-lined studies

or cough 'til our lungs give up their longings.

Which is to say, we must receive.

So here's to giving.

Adam Relates the
Last Days of Rome

That night even our dinner wore formal attire,
though the toilets wouldn't flush, and the napkins
were rags, and what water we had was a kind of brine.

As the crowds amassed at the doors we dined
through the over-there din of an iron-age Strat
and its three torn chords, while the Barbars,

in a show of virility, threw at each other
their tattooed selves. What can't be eaten
burns. What doesn't burn, sells. What won't

be sold we've leaned against the gates.
We pierced our daughters. We taught them to smoke.
They entered the mob with a kind of grace.

Adam Explains the Origin

After the city of ash and sulfur; After the fall
to the dark of the lake; After all
the wrong angels had baked into age,
the good lord, they say, got lonely, lonely...

Dead-dog and sweet-Lucy-done-left-me lonely.
Rogue-cosmonaut-lost-in-the-vacuum lonely. And so
he built a beast of earth that wouldn't bark
or bite, that fawned, that had no spite
boiling in it like bile, a thing
that he could tickle on its little head at night
before bedding down in a heap of stars—

Lucy, he wanted to make it right.
He wanted to make another you. He wanted to do
it all over but you,
        you skulked through the night
to tongue your double's ear;
you taught it to fight, to flirt, to steal cars.

        What is it we fear
the dead might do, tiptoeing like thieves
through the brain's back yard?
        What is it we want
when we make of the living the ones we've lost?

        God missed the dead.
He brought them back.
        And that's the cost.

Red Shift

*... it was found that distant stars were all shifted toward the
red end of the visible spectrum, a Doppler effect that meant
those galaxies were moving away from our own, ... and that
the size of a galaxy's red shift was directly proportional to its
distance. In other words, the farther a galaxy is, the faster it
is moving away.* —Stephen Hawking

Everything was moving away from me.

Andromeda was moving away from me,
Sirius was moving away from me;

Flight 814, trailing its benign white streamer
of smoke—away from me. And my voice
was moving away from me, mingling in
with the airport's breakneck, anxious din.

My father's death was moving away from me—
becoming darker, becoming cooler,
becoming the widest color of light
that won't expose the reel; and the reel,
too, was moving away from me:
the scene ballooning, blurring, until the screen
held a blue-green square of the gurney,
a quadrant of freckles mapped on an arm.

◆ ◆ ◆

Of all the meanings of *exposed* I think my favorite
is the raw nerve shivering bug-like in the lamp light
while the surgeon arranges his dainty knives.

You can get close to that. You can brush
its wriggling limb and hear the scream.

You can lie there on the table, say,
"little nerve oh nerve it'll
be all right; there
there, there there."

◆ ◆ ◆

The following question is worth 100 points:

If Sean Bishop is sitting on the wing
of a Boeing 727, flying
381 miles per hour due east,

and Ron Bishop's on an Airbus A320
cruising due west at equivalent speed,

by how much must either decelerate to hear
how brightly the maples, this year, are burning?

◆ ◆ ◆

At Gate 2A I did the math,
I traced the sorry origins.

Relative as in "the relatives
have canceled the family Christmas."

Relative as in meaningless
when alone or apart.

Relative as in the state of rest
is relative, as in distance is relative,
while the speed of light is absolute.

Therefore time, and space.
Therefore my father's death is a place
its citizens can't return to,
where the water runs black,
where a lost flock of starlings
moves smoke-like and sentient over the grasses.

◆ ◆ ◆

Maine Medical ICU, room 2
8/14/08, 8:30 PM.

Portland International Jetport, Gate 2A.
1/12/09, 9:20 AM.

Here and now. Wherever I am
today, among some things, some faces.

One of me lives in each of these places.
One of me lives, and none of him.

Adam Reports from the Distant Future

To the old terrors were added the new terrors.

Still the coat rack in half-sleep looked like a body.
Still the cicada woke saddened in its caved-in mine.
And the white threads wriggled awfully in the litter box,
the search party came back carrying a shoe.

When at long last the Idea of the Individual collapsed
some were given four arms and some got none.
Haphazardly were distributed the world's humble sufferings

but so too the lotto winnings, and you looked so beautiful
in your new scarf and that lipstick of an as-yet-unachievable-
by-twenty-first-century-chemistry red.

We entered the café called The Garden where The Garden
two hundred thousand years back used to be,
and asked for our usual table.

I put my hand to your cheek,
and my other hand to your other cheek,
and with my other two hands I helped you pray:

"Lord," you said, "I would like to remove
about twelve billion people from the world—
in this way I grow more like You every day."

2

Black Hole Owners Association

Hello. And welcome to One-of-Us,
    however you came to be. Maybe one trailed you
        to the highway's charitable din, when,
            lost at dusk in a Texan swamp, you discovered it
                like a marvelous and terrifying orchid.
Maybe you're a boy with a bucket of pond water
or alternately a grown man honestly in love,
    and you've learned at last that your tadpole is a minnow
    or the woman in question will never grow to love you,
        causing a grain-sized singularity to pearl itself
        at the center of your disappointment.
It could be that you are very very ill
    and there it was one day, a pill among the others;
or someone died—maybe it was discovered
    at the scattering: a marble in the empty urn.

Whatever the cause, though: welcome, welcome.
    There are things we feel you need to know:
You should name it, of course, but please don't name it
    Regret or Oblivion or Sadness or Hurt
    From Which I Suspect I Will Never Recover.
        "Oh Sadness," you might say, "come lie
            with me in bed for an hour
            while the moon takes off its dress."
        Or: "Oh Oblivion, you've made such an awful mess
            of things again."
You shouldn't encourage it. You shouldn't feed it,

either, though it will seem to ask to be fed,
bending the space around its bowl—

Don't give it a bowl. Don't get too close. Your black hole
is going to take a lot of time; time will nearly stop,
in fact, in its vicinity. You will sleep for days
without knowing. Your minutes
will be your neighbors' hours.
"What did you do this week?"
your friends will ask, and you will say
you ate breakfast
or bought a t-shirt at the mall
or sampled that new flavor-changing gum
while their lives will seem an impossible bustle
of joy and actual achievements.

Like a tortoise, your black hole will outlive you.
You will pass it on. Already
you should think of your small patch of darkness
as the darkness of your children. Late into the night and alone,
they will run their grownup hands along its outer regions
and be reminded of you.
Take comfort in that—though you are right to feel pity.
Your black hole, after all, is a sort of hell
that sulks in the corner and churns and churns
and renders all the nightlights useless when,
groggy and dream-spooked, your children rise from bed to pee.

We're sorry that by necessity we will never meet you.
On one of your walks, should you see another walker

with an impossible dimple of emptiness straining at its chain,
feel free to wave but please do not approach—

all tooth and gullet and terrible maw,
you have no idea what they would do to one another.

Letter to Toss from the Airborne Plane

Dear dead dad: a birdlike therapist
demanded of me this letter. It's winter:

out on the tarmac sleet cakes the wings
of the morning's latest delays

and the terminal's filling with bodies and bodies
that only want to go. Outside Gate 2A,

the mechanics have wrenched a gear from the plane,
squabbled, locked up, and walked off.

And this is why I thought of you today:
how the surgeons sighed and argued;

how your brain, like an injured animal, sulked
and told them nothing. Tomorrow

it could be a branch the width of your wrist
that reminds me, the cleft in a stranger's chin,

or a food stain blooming in the cookbook you left.
Since you can't ask,

I'll tell you the turkey was burnt this year,
that your brother (for once) wasn't such an ass,

that the wishbone wouldn't break in half,
but thirds, the top part flying off

into the chocolate mousse.
So what's that mean? somebody laughed,

and I said, *both of us lose.*

Secret Fellow Sufferers,

our fathers are liars:
Some slick beast is breathing by our bedsides.
Down the chimney each winter a dead saint comes
to cough into our hearths a year of obligations.
And the scratch at our window is not just the birch.
And the watermelon seeds have taken root inside us.

In the old dream, I hopped a train
and then woke to its real-world warning,
believing a piece of me was lost to some cargo
bound for Tacoma, where rain
is more than a mood.
                            And it was.

The world is too large.
You can wander it, looking,
and not possibly find it.

Of all the voices you hear,
one must be your father's. It asks,

What are you looking for? What
are *you* looking for? What are
you looking *for*?

What I Asked For

Grown   woman   just learning

to whistle,   tuneless.   Half-steeped

in sleep,   I thought she was   the kettle

debating   doneness.   She was

naked, a grown   woman,   whistling and

frying tomatoes—   the white   brindle

on her hips   where her hips   were in

a hurry. To be   done. To be   done with.

To be a grown   woman   looking back

on the cities that   bore her,   the white

brindle the brindle   of a big cat,   of something

slinking   in a bleached   prairie, looking back

on an oasis—and so   far to go yet.   I was

a city looked   back on. I asked   for a grown

woman; I got   an animal.   And an animal

doesn't know what   it wants until   the wanting

becomes it.   She had woken   too early wanting

tomatoes.   I had thought she   was a kettle debating

doneness; I had thought   she was a grown   woman. I

was wrong; I was   done with.   She was looking

back.   Looking back,   she was salt, was

a pillar. Already   the kettle had found   its tune, was done with   searching.   It wouldn't

stop   until the house   burned, until

the salt in the   shape of a grown   woman had

melted in   steam, had streamed   out the door

to seed   the garden. As if   the tomatoes could be

done with, could be   salted before   they grew.

A grown   woman.   I asked, as a child

for an animal   and got one: A dog. I

named it   Dog. It wanted   all the tomatoes

from the garden and   got them,   and got

sick on the floor. I   cleaned it up.   I am

learning.   When next I am asked   I will ask

for my   fields filled   with salt. I will

ask   for a salt lick.   The animals will

travel for   miles. They won't   know what

they want,   until   they want me.

Secret Fellow Sufferers,

once I believed if I wore my sadness
like a fine suit I'd one day grow into, I'd seem
an old sage of the fashionable love
for the day-before-yesterday's smart tomorrow.

Then it was today. My tie looked terrible
in its decatriplet Windsor, frayed as a noose.
I wanted a dog, wanted all my belongings
tied up in a hanky on a new, red caboose
but they don't make cabooses anymore.

My lady waved a white veil from the dining car.
It was 1897; it was 3094.
The world had given up on love. And war.

On Believing the Night
Has an End When
the Night Has No End

The quarterback spits in his shoe and believes
therefore he'll win today.

                    In this story
I am the believing, though once I thought
I was the shoe; I thought my father
was the spit; I thought
                    the quarterback
was very bearded and flanked
by handsome cherubim in helmets
and protective gear.

                    What luck
to live in a physics of entropy,
blitzed by the blank light
of the disc we spin in
and will spin out of—it means

            we can think, if we want,
that the future stands before us like a preacher
on the sidewalk, waving his stack
of shoddy bibles, though it does not.

            We can think we could do anything today
but we won't do anything today.

We can think we'd be better off
for being able to do something we don't
want to do, if we wanted to.

Less vaguely,
I mean I admire the shrew
lost on the astroturf, which doesn't dream
of one day being the senior broker
it won't be.

Less vaguely still,
I am talking to *you*—whom I haven't
even told yet, in this story, what to win is.

Secret Fellow Sufferers,

once more our old wounds
like milkweed pods have opened, and we're lovely again

as our winces break off in the wind.
When the mailman comes with his bright bouquet

of unbeatable deals, I'll invite him in
and tend to his blisters. I will ask if he thinks

in the end, when the heart monitor blips its sonar
for the distance between here and gone, I mean—

what will he want the most: a hand to hold
or a mojito?, a blowjob or a prosaic

declaration of spiritual love? We must identify
the ones of us who've lived whole years

with a wasp in their mouths, and our enemies
who believe the trick to ascending

to a bright hereafter is to tread so lightly
they float away—as if to give oneself to the wind

doesn't require breaking apart, until
each piece of you seems ethereal and strange.

Secret Fellow Sufferers,

have you been the unwinged thing
perched and testing the phone wire's teeter?

Have you weighed the big Pro against the many feathery Cons?
Have you watched the brows of standers-below

as they fell into wish from honest worry?
Sometimes the wind off the lake sounds like a siren

approaching your rescue, instead of the air
asking unanswered for someone to stop it.

Sometimes you think, well, if you were just
a mild-mannered raindrop softly plummeting you'd get

to be a part again of the fat puddle that made you,
when really you'd just be a raindrop with a raindrop's

usual worries, stuck for good among the others
who had, like you, such higher hopes than this.

At The Optometrist's I Almost Remember a Story I've Almost Remembered Before

My father had one thumbnail like a fossil—
scalloped, marbled yellow, a slug print trapped in lime.

"Canning factory," the story went. "Conveyor belt."
And as he told it, he'd rub the nail

as if to smooth it out, or as if the script
were written there in Braille.

If the scientists are right, eventually all we have
to remember with are bodies:

"The teeth of children," a waiting-room magazine declares,
"are among the most prized of finds,"

meaning we can tell how big
at what age, famine or drought,

whether the parents were cruel or kind.
Each time I heard the story I knew

to be a man meant to suffer
undeservedly, and so I'd never be a man

like that, with a gnarled proof to teach

people how to fear—to be made

of a hurt until that hurt became a badge
I learned to pin to others.

In the exam, the optometrist looks into my pupil,
looks into me and tells me

that my lens has a long, old tear,
probably from head trauma as a child,

which is something I've been told
by every optometrist for a decade

but keep forgetting. I don't remember
any trauma. What I do

is my father: how when he was ashamed,
or sorry, he'd tuck his mangled nail into his palm,

as if he were an archaeologist trying to re-bury
the discovery of an ancestor we shouldn't be proud of;

as if what he wanted most was to walk away
from the place he found it, where soon

the dust would make, again, of the past
a world he wouldn't need to recognize.

Theory of Cruelty

Though fit for soup, the snapper-turtle
that gnaws your finger won't let go.
And though a sunfish cuddles even to a hook

dropped bare in the lake, and is beautiful, it dries
on the hot dock where the boys leave it flopping.
If you believe in Somebody, then Somebody

made a rule: to choose between muck-dark
hunger and kindness, which glints in the light
while above, the redtails trace the shape

of longing and forever. —Check your watch:
someone in robes and bones right now
is trying the limits of never killing, a young monk

grows wiser by being beaten, and the dodoes
in their books have learned too late
but learned, at least, that love

is not the answer. I wanted to tell you,
today, we don't know
which side of the quiet war will win—
                            We know.

Lake Bobby

In the town of boots and church and barter
and the pull-tooth barber gabbing dust and corn,
one day among the talkers, like fog, came a worry:
a deep drought, yet the old quarry filled with water.
They called in the experts, who shrugged. It blackened:
No rain and no spring, but the black lake rose.
The preacher thought, *this changes everything*—he sat;
he couldn't preach or speak; light panned over the pews.
Still, the congregation grew: they were a canvas for the light.
They were the flock of the waiting, and they loved the lord so.

So the quarry filled three inches, and three more each day,
until it bulged pupil-dark at the brim, then stopped.
The preacher grew morose; he wanted poison so he drank it.
But he lived, and he lived, and it became the new communion.
Then the state laid pipe: the new clear was black.
And the church swelled, too, through the stores and houses.
The lake seemed to grow, but didn't spill—it stretched—
and the surveyors measured and muttered confusions:
it was a quick walk around, but they couldn't see across.
So they all became deacons; they took the collection.

Soon the children grew silent and wild and more brave.
They looked at each other, and each other understood.
They made a couple sandwiches, they found planks for paddles,
then dragged out a dinghy to set on the water.
The straws were arranged and they drew: it was Bobby.

So they grinned and they waved; Bobby paddled away.

Brave Bobby whose boat sits still on the lake.

Bobby whose voice floats, still, on the waves.

Oh daughters and sons of the church, let us pray.

3

TO THROW THE LITTLE BONES THAT SPEAK

Who's here for rest from every pain or ill? Who's here for Lethe's plain? the Donkey shearings? Cerberia? Taenarum? or the Ravens? . . . Step in. . . . Just dip your oar in once, you'll hear the loveliest timing songs.

—Aristophanes, from *The Frogs*

I

Jack of Hearts, Jack of the weakest ventricle:
I'm saving this dance for the boatlady Karen.

Play me the one about the starving Danish stowaway
welcomed to shore by a conflagration.

When the pointman plays squeezebox in the murk and grime,
when the band chimes in on their sitars and lyres,

make believe it isn't over. Pretend there's time
to woo the wrinkled weavers away from their nets.

Oh Jack. Oh Karen. Oh keepers of gates,
I've built you a toy out of bones and regrets.

Please accept this offering as a lamb,
bleating in the chest before the awful rattle.

II

Let's say the heebie-jeebies are a kind of flea
and the underbed shadows are only dust.

Let's play the game where there is no death.
Let's trust the few signs that we're still alive:

soul sloshing like backwash in the breathing body,
this cat's incessant scotchbrite kiss,

the old bread growing out its fur.
Will we miss the stamped planet of expirations?

Jack, in the cold black bog, we tire
of you: our aortal ache—what remains

of a child's body with its breakable bones,
of how many licks until we hit the marrow.

III

My little hooked pickerels, just look
what I can offer.

Far from here where the smog is cooler,
they'll pour you a pond you can call your own:

some musty woods and their choir of toads,
the petty carnages of beetles,

one lone surviving Pangaean iris.
I hereby propose

this trade for nothing:
a forever-long stay in the blacker lake.

The presiding angel demanding softly,
please don't go.

IV

Edge of the bright earth
where we say the dead *pass*, like it's high-school science—

Can't we admit the body's a boat
where its own undoings bob through the day?

To what end, anyway: this dreaming of woods
and a tireless choir of toads

who hop far off where the smog is cooler;
this dreaming of black bogs

where the roasted geese can roost forever.
Little pickerels, in the towns of the living

the leaves have started falling
and you're going to have to choose.

V

The last—give or take—forever I've spent
betting at morning against the light

while the barb and bobber, the line and bough
strafe the muck all day. Tonight

I'm cozying up to eternity
among the nonbelievers—all scales

and gills, no knees for kneeling—
to drift and drift in the dotted dark

to which you've given me,
Karen. You toss the keys

to every passenger. You give
each one a kiss. You disappear.

VI

Ladies and gents, if you look to your left
you'll see the soft glow of approaching lava,

the petty carnages of beetles,
the sad king/crooner who tends the bridge.

What seems. What is. What wriggles and feeds.
Just like the herdsman I want to believe

in one big moon in the bigger sky,
to give myself up like a plucked bud

to all who've come to find me,
wherever I am. Somebody tell me,

where is Karen. Who are these tourists
pressing pennies in my hand.

VII

From a list of great evils I've chosen the best:
to beat the dog for being fearful,

to bet at dusk against the dark,
and the heart, the idiot heart

that fails. In the towns
of the living the leaves have fallen

like sheets from the bitter writ of birds.
A quiz, little pickerels: how do we think

the dusk pulls shut the shade of night,
and why do we call for it? What do we want?

A peck. An eye. An iris.
A promise of more.

VIII

Karen you promised you'd come but didn't
so I've captained this cardboard skiff through the night.

City of Cherubim, City of Dis,
one is the sorriest digit that beats.

The rudder's gone soggy,
the lake's at my feet,

in the air no sound but the sound of air.
Just like the herdsman I want to believe

in one big moon in the bigger sky,
to love the middle world and its imperfections:

these six warped chords on endless loop;
E as in Everything, T as in Tomorrow.

4

Secret Fellow Sufferers,

please join me in compiling
some likenesses to the night we're not sleeping in:

Is it the craze of mange in an uncle's hound
or is it a black tick fattening with worry?

It might be my imagination of the funeral suit, dangling
from the actually-empty hanger on the closet door,

or the tarmac where the jets aren't right now dozing
with their engines ticking like hallway clocks.

This night could be the dock on the night
of the lake's first freezing. It could be the frost

making glass of the water. It could be the fish peering through
at the stars, which could be swiftly falling knives.

Remember the day you loved somebody best
was the day you were dying and the doctors shined up

their syringes to prove if the rumors were true.
If it's for fear that you're not sleeping, remember

that fear taken far enough leads to fainting,
so recall the needle hilt-deep in your marrow

and the morphine after, like a low sweet song.
Next time, when it's over, you will be alone.

Secret Fellow Sufferers,

some of us
are cured. How terrible

to be suddenly well in the dayglo world
with one's shaker of pills

like kaleidoscopic jewels, among
so many unbearable beauties.

If like me you are lucky,
when the old hurt lifts you'll be left,

at least, with the hate you'd half-forgotten
in the woods behind your teenage home.

It may look like a heron in the brook.
It may iridesce like weird lichen in the night.

You might keep it as a trinket on your desk
at the Office of Sufferers' Internal Affairs,

where with a sense of pride and duty
of which previously you were incapable

you will find and revoke the privileges of
the horrible, the healed.

Joe Cuomo, Local Weatherman, Tests the Old Idea of Heaven

That the goldfinch yellows further for the grasses.
That the trenches in dawnlight grow a little darker.
That the day before my father's death

was National Skinny Dipping Day, Filet
Mignon Day, and Left Hander's Day. And the day
he made his last, accidental utterance—first a hush

like the flame going out on a stove, then a rasp
and low vowel, as if he were a radio station we'd lost
to static, winding through the mountains—

was National Creamsicle Day. So in the Somewhere
the Breyer's Ice Cream factory calls home, the children
of Somewhere Elementary were sugared and giddy

on the day the doctor warned me that when his toes
began to curl, or when his arms began to swell
and warm, and tighten, it meant the end.

In a nearby field, the people of Lewiston, Maine
were preparing for Hot Air Balloon Day: the nylon shapes
of cartoon heroes draped across the grasses,

as if flattened by anvils and ready
to shake themselves back to standing. All night,

like TV personalities in the lit squares of their windows,

the children surveyed the field where the blue lights
of the burners puffed on and off. Come morning,
before the wind picked up, anachronistic and brave

in his wicker basket, local weatherman Joe Cuomo
set out to prophecy the day, while in front of their TVs
the children hoped to get a look at heaven,

but instead got a weatherman
remarking on the elephantine weight of the clouds.
This is how it works: wonder, then loss,

and then new wonder. I knew
that without me, my father would be trapped
in the wet heft of his body.

And so, untethered from the machines
standing by like awestruck spectators,
my father huffed the last heat inside him

while outside, a day early, the first
impatient balloon shoved off,
and made the blue sky bluer by its redness.

About to Hope

My sky'd go green if I had a sky; its birds
would shut their beaks already. *About to*

must begin like that, like *I don't know
what else to be, let's be it*. Soon

you're dragging your black spout
through Oklahoma; you're wriggling

loose of your own wrecked womb.
You don't get to choose

if you're the doctor, if your ass gets slapped
and slick with goo, if you lie splayed

with what used to be a piece of you
missing, and making demands. Whichever

way, it's something new: You'll know me
by my egg tooth—how I arrive

at the barbecue, all wrong, in my suit
of fine wool, in the storm's wet havoc.

It starts that way—boo hoo, boo hoo—
you're dressed for fun like someone died,

when the funnel lifts: shaken
martinis fall out of the sky.

Secret Fellow Sufferers,

I've come a long way
to the pulpit today to advance our causes:

No more coal-mine canaries. Abolish Susan Jeffries
who teases Max Biggins who sits on the seesaw

and cries and cries. May she admit
she wants to marry him; may the foremen confess

that oft in the dark and brute weight of their debts
they ruffle their feathers and start to sing.

Citizens, Parishioners, have you ever been dying?
I have. It's a fairly shitty business—the way

the doctors unpack the latest devices
to hurt you by heretofore impossible means.

I move to declare our headaches, today,
a national emergency. May the Guard

provide Max Biggins with a box of tissues.
We simply won't rest until the Marines

emerge from the caves with their hands in prayer,
each holding within him a faint and frantic chirping.

Last Supper
Uffizi Gallery Exhibit, Chazen Museum, 2012

The bread on the table becomes the table.

The dishes depart. The goblets
leave their wine mid-air, in orbit
of the boy asleep beside Christ, after Christ

has become two stripped sticks
propped on a hill,

has become a word, has become a word
for that word, until his name
might as well be Ambulance
or Penicillin.

◆ ◆ ◆

The wrong kind of saving is still saving.

You take out your camera
on the dark riverbank, after the bridge
has grown too tired to stand,
while the barges capsize in the tumult,
while the headlights blink out
two by two underwater.

Or you announce to a room full of strangers:
once, you sat in a hospital beside your father

until he was a gallon of breath
inching unseen toward the ventilation,
until he was a sheet, was a stain
in the shape of himself
the nurses took away.

◆ ◆ ◆

The body on the table becomes the table.

You're still the boy asleep at dinner
until you wake as a prophet in an empty room
where the painting you're a part of has begun to fade.

And the doctors have some papers for you to sign.

And the papers want to know why you just stood there
while the townspeople drowned.

And the townspeople, and your father, they want to know—
will it be the way you say it will: mostly fire
and a hurt that won't stop?

◆ ◆ ◆

What you know is what you dreamed.

You imagine a Graceland
where the televisions play
side by side, as if speaking
to one another; as if someone
still lives there.

Or a mansion in Massachusetts
where Dickinson's dress
floats, a ghost boxed in glass.

◆ ◆ ◆

You try to remember.
You can't remember.

The body on the table that becomes the table
might still be a body somewhere

in a high-tech crematorium
that burns so clean it doesn't cough
the white smoke of the Vatican that means
"he is among us," or the black smoke
that means "we don't know,"

but a vapor, clear
as air, meaning something
you can't name. Meaning some
kind of saving.

Notes Toward Basic Betterness

The way the anglerfish might rather be
just the light it hangs in the Atlantic night,

or the moon might want to live as only
the cloistered stones adored by NASA,

today in this inner-life dusk I'd like
to become a smaller, simpler portion of myself.

Pretty soon now the day will dim down
to its little black dress and slink toward darker needs,

lurching high-heeled with a cruel thug 'til dawn
and smashing all the neighbors' windows.

For once, inner bitterness, I think I'd like
not to forgive it, exactly, but at least allow its fact—

the way the girl burned by the bombings learns
to live only among her basic beauties,

and not the way the pilot opening the hatch
inhabited entirely the motive for the war.

What today wants, maybe, is no part of itself
at all, but the idea of its dayness,

like the couple in bed who want so much
to be for an hour the space they've built between them.

How every atom envies light.
How the moon, now that I think of it,

might rather be the golf ball abandoned on its surface,
or one just like it: a dimpled concept of itself

the people of Earth can hold and consider,
so it might feel at last what I

am feeling for you right now,
secret reader.

NOTES

"Adam Before the Advent of Psychiatry" is based in part on an apocryphal Biblical text called *The Book of Adam and Eve*.

The epigraph of "Red Shift" takes small liberties for the sake of clarity and concision; the full, exact text appears in *A Brief History of Time*.

The title "To Throw the Little Bones that Speak" refers to the origins of the *I Ching*. The sequence was drafted by randomly selecting good lines from otherwise failed poems, and then writing the remainder of each section around those lines.

"About to Hope" is for Rebecca Hazelton.

"Last Supper" was written in response to an art exhibit titled "Offerings from the Angels," featuring paintings and tapestries from the Uffizi Gallery.

ACKNOWLEDGMENTS

Profound thanks to my family, friends, and writer colleagues, not all of whom can be listed here: Samuel Amadon, Amy Quan Barry, Seth Bishop, Amelia Bucek, Kara Candito, Chuck Carlise, Laurie Ann Cedilnik, Hayan Charara, Lydia Conklin, Judy Coombs, Liz Countryman, Adam Day, Sneha Desai, Mark Doty, Ryler Dustin, Eric Ekstrand, Laura Eve Engel, Lydia Fitzpatrick, Nick Flynn, Zaccaria Fulton, Hannah Gamble, Kasten Glover, Sarah Gubbins, Daniel Hall, Rebecca Hazelton, Eric Higgins, Tony Hoagland, Sterling Holywhitemountain, Paul Jenkins, Amaud Jamaul Johnson, Janine Joseph, Anna Journey, Jesse Lee Kercheval, Eric Kocher, Ron Kuka, Brandon Lopez, Kerb Lydick, Sam Mak, Judith Claire Mitchell, Rachael Morrison, Andrew Mortazavi, Hannah Oberman-Breindel, Yuko Sakata, Martha Serpas, Glenn Shaheen, Kent Shaw, Bruce Smith, Liz Waldner, Ron Wallace, Michael West, and Nancy Yaffe.

Thanks also to Susan Mitchell, Sarah Gorham, Kirby Gann, Kristen Radtke, Megan Bowden, Jeffrey Skinner, and everyone at Sarabande.

Many of these poems were written with the support of the Wisconsin Institute for Creative Writing's Diane Middlebrook Poetry Fellowship, the Poetry Foundation's Ruth Lilly Fellowship, the University of Houston, and several scholarships and prizes from Inprint–Houston.

Finally, thanks to the following journals, in which these poems initially appeared: *Alaska Quarterly Review* ("Adam Reports from the Distant Future," "Black Hole Owners Association," "Secret Fellow Sufferers, [once more our old wounds]," and "Secret Fellow Sufferers, [some of us are cured]"); *Bat City Review* ("Lake Bobby"); *Carolina Quarterly* ("Notes Toward Basic Betterness"); *Connotation Press* ("To Throw the Little Bones that Speak"); *Forklift Ohio* ("A Bit of Forgiveness" and "Adam Home from the Wars"); *Harvard Review* ("Terms of Service"); *Hayden's Ferry Review* ("Here's to Killing" and "Adam Explains the Origin"); *Indiana Review* ("Adam Before the Advent of Psychiatry" and "Adam Explains His Implications"); *The Nashville Review* ("Joe Cuomo, Local Weatherman, Tests the Old Idea of Heaven"); *Ninth Letter* ("Letter to Toss from the Airborne Plane"); *Ploughshares* ("Secret Fellow Sufferers, [I've come a long way]" and "Secret Fellow Sufferers, [have you been the unwinged thing]"); and *Salt Hill* ("Reading Dante in the ICU" and "Red Shift").

SEAN BISHOP lives in Madison, Wisconsin, where he teaches creative writing and creative writing pedagogy and coordinates the MFA and Fellowship programs at the University of Wisconsin–Madison. He received his MFA from the University of Houston, where he was the managing editor of *Gulf Coast* from 2008–2010. He is the founding editor of *Better* (bettermagazine.org).

THE KATHRYN A. MORTON PRIZE IN POETRY

2013 — SEAN BISHOP
The Night We're Not Sleeping In,
selected by Susan Mitchell

TREY MOODY — 2012
Thought That Nature,
selected by Cole Swensen

2011 — LAUREN SHAPIRO
Easy Math, selected by
Marie Howe

DAVID HERNANDEZ — 2010
Hoodwinked, selected by
Amy Gerstler

2009 — JULIA STORY
Post Moxie, selected by
Dan Chiassonn

KARYNA MCGLYNN — 2008
*I Have to Go Back to 1994 and Kill
a Girl*, selected by Lynn Emanuel

2007 — MONICA FERRELL
Beasts for the Chase,
selected by Jane Hirshfield

GABRIEL FRIED — 2006
Making the New Lamb Take,
selected by Michael Ryan

2005 — MATTHEW LIPPMAN
The New Year of Yellow,
selected by Tony Hoagland

SIMONE MUENCH — 2004
Lampblack and Ash, selected by
Carol Muske-Dukes

2003 — KAREN AN-HWEI LEE
In Medias Res, selected by
Heather McHugh

CARRIE ST. GEORGE COMER — 2002
The Unrequited, selected by
Stephen Dunn

2001 — RICK BAROT
The Darker Fall, selected by
Stanley Plumly

CATE MARVIN — 2000
World's Tallest Disaster,
selected by Robert Pinsky

1999 — DEBORAH TALL
Summons, selected by
Charles Simic

ALEIDA RODRIGUEZ — 1998
Garden of Exile, selected by
Marilyn Hacker

1997 — JAMES KIMBRELL
The Gatehouse Heaven,
selected by Charles Wright

BARON WORMSER — 1996
When, selected by
Alice Fulton

1995 — JANE MEAD
*The Lord and the General Din of
the World*, selected by Philip Levine

ABOUT SARABANDE

Sarabande Books thanks you for the purchase of this collection; we do hope you enjoy it! Founded in 1994 as an independent, nonprofit, literary press, Sarabande publishes poetry, short fiction, and literary nonfiction—genres increasingly neglected by commercial publishers. We are committed to producing beautiful, lasting editions that honor exceptional writing, and to keeping those books in print. If you're interested in further reading, take a moment to browse our website, sarabandebooks.org. There you'll find information about other titles; opportunities to contribute to the Sarabande mission; and an abundance of supporting materials including audio, video, a lively blog, and our Sarabande in Education program.